BOOK 1

Jazz, Rags & Blues

D1367219

10 original pieces for the late elementary to early intermediate pianist

MARTHA MIER

FOREWORD

Jazz is an important and distinctive American contribution to 20th-century music. *Jazz, Rags and Blues,* Book One, contains ten original solos that reflect the various styles of the jazz idiom. From the mournful blues sound in "Don't Wanna' Leave You Blues," to the driving, syncopated rhythm in "A Neat Beat," students will love the challenge of playing in the jazz style.

Jazz is fun to play! Students will be inspired and motivated by the syncopated rhythms and the colorful, rich harmonies of jazz—a style which has captured the imagination of performer and listener alike!

CONTENTS

Don't Wanna' Leave You Blues. 4
Downright Happy Rag. 18
Hallelujah!. 8
Just Struttin' Along 2
Neat Beat, A. 21
Ol' Rockin' Chair Blues 10
Ragtime Do-si-do 6
Seventh Street Blues 14
Sneaky Business. 16
Surfboard Boogie 12

ISBN-10: 0-7390-0963-X (Book) ISBN-10: 0-7390-7528-4 (Book & CD)
ISBN-13: 978-0-7390-0963-5 (Book) ISBN-13: 978-0-7390-7528-9 (Book & CD)

Alfred

A General MIDI disk is available (14423), which includes a full piano recording and background accompaniment.

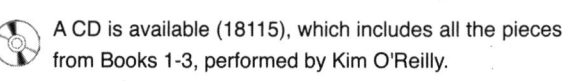

A CD is available (18115), which includes all the pieces from Books 1-3, performed by Kim O'Reilly.

Just Struttin' Along

Moderate blues swing (♫ = ♩ ♪ triplet)

Martha Mier

13
mf
16
f
19
8va
mp
22
p
8va
mp
(no rit.)
(LH)
pp

Don't Wanna' Leave You Blues

Mournfully, with slow blues swing (♫ = ♩ ♪ triplet)
(♩ = 80)

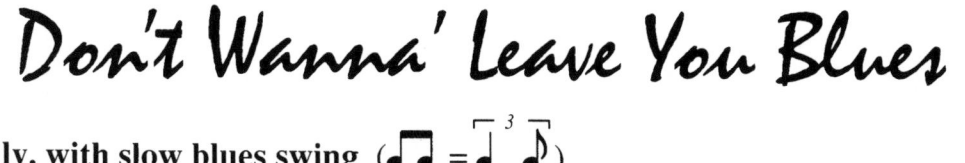

Martha Mier

12
1
3
1
mf
15
18
1
2
3
4
3
5
3
1
2
mp
3
21
3
rit.
p
1
2
5

Ragtime Do-si-do

Fast, spirited (Play ♪♪ evenly)

Martha Mier

17
mf
21
25
mp
29
f
33
mp
f

Hallelujah!

Happily, with spirit (Play ♩♫ evenly)

Martha Mier

13
mf
16
f
20
23
rit.
p
pp
8va

Ol' Rockin' Chair Blues

Unhurried, slow blues swing (♪♪ = ♩ ♪ in a triplet)
(♩ = 80)

Martha Mier

13
16
20
23
26
mp
rit.

Surfboard Boogie

Martha Mier

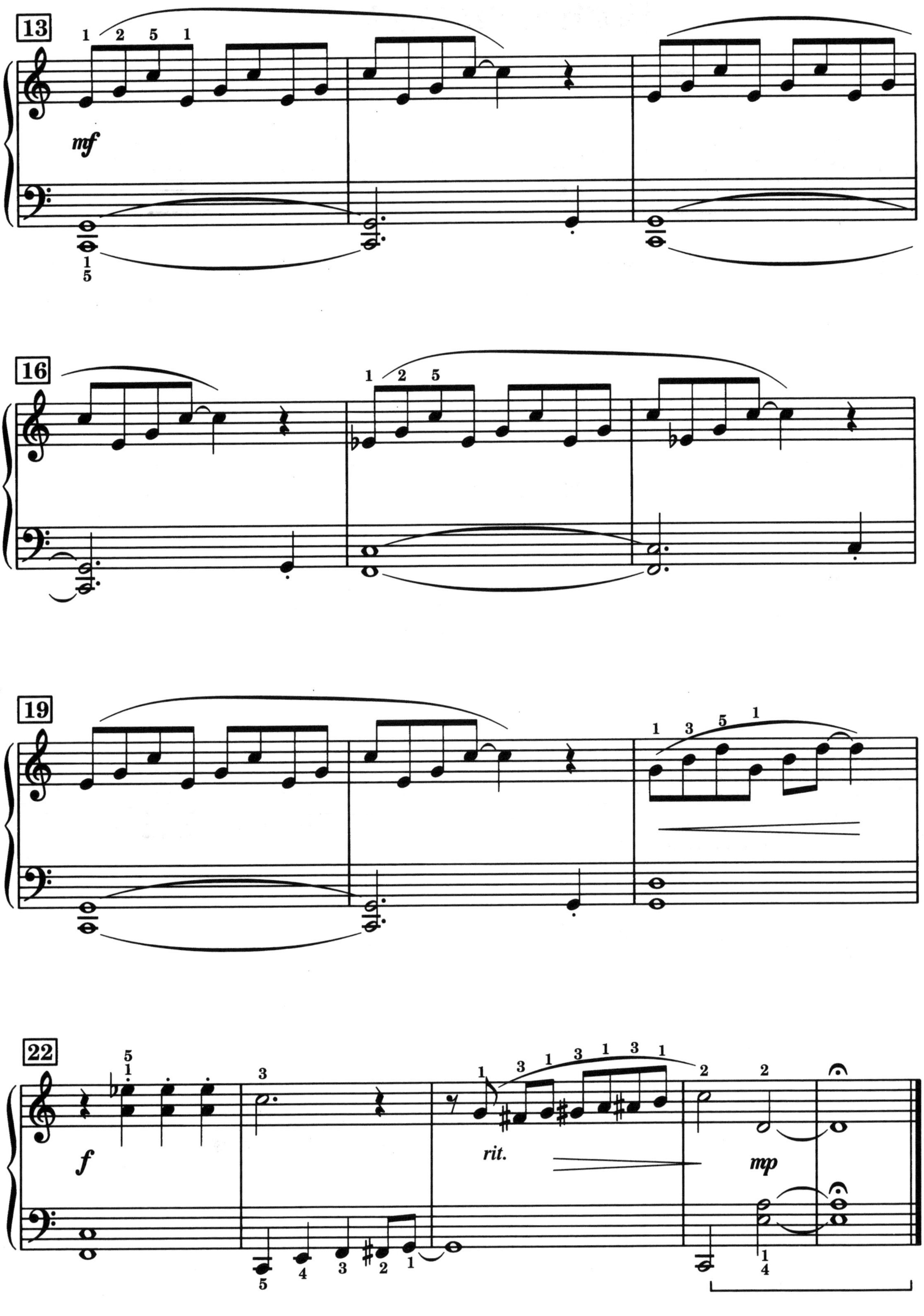
13
mf
16
19
22
f
rit.
mp

Seventh Street Blues

Slowly, wistfully (Play ♩♪ evenly)
(♩ = 88)

Martha Mier

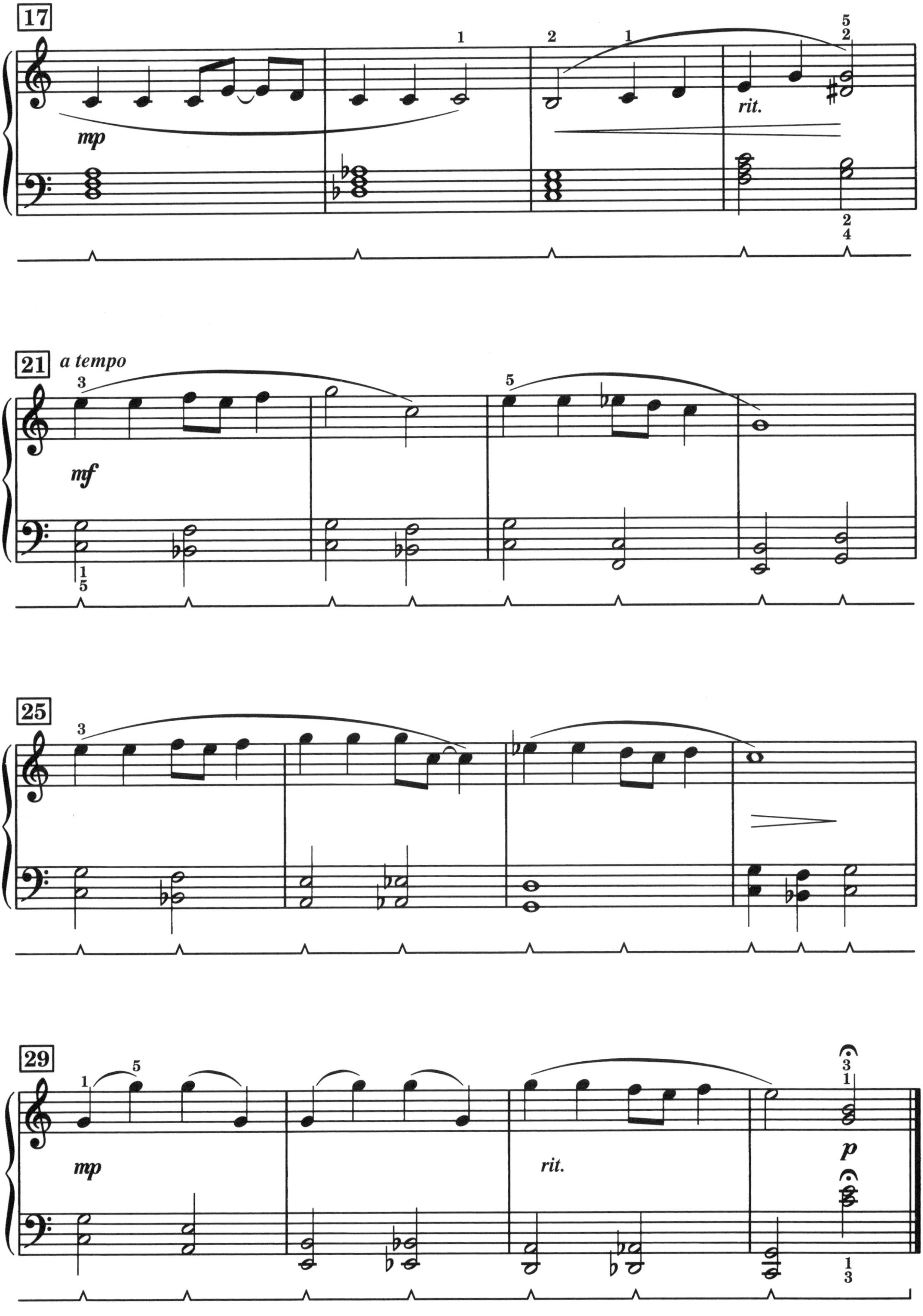
17
mp
rit.
21
a tempo
mf
25
29
rit.
p

Sneaky Business

Martha Mier

Allegro (♩ = 132)

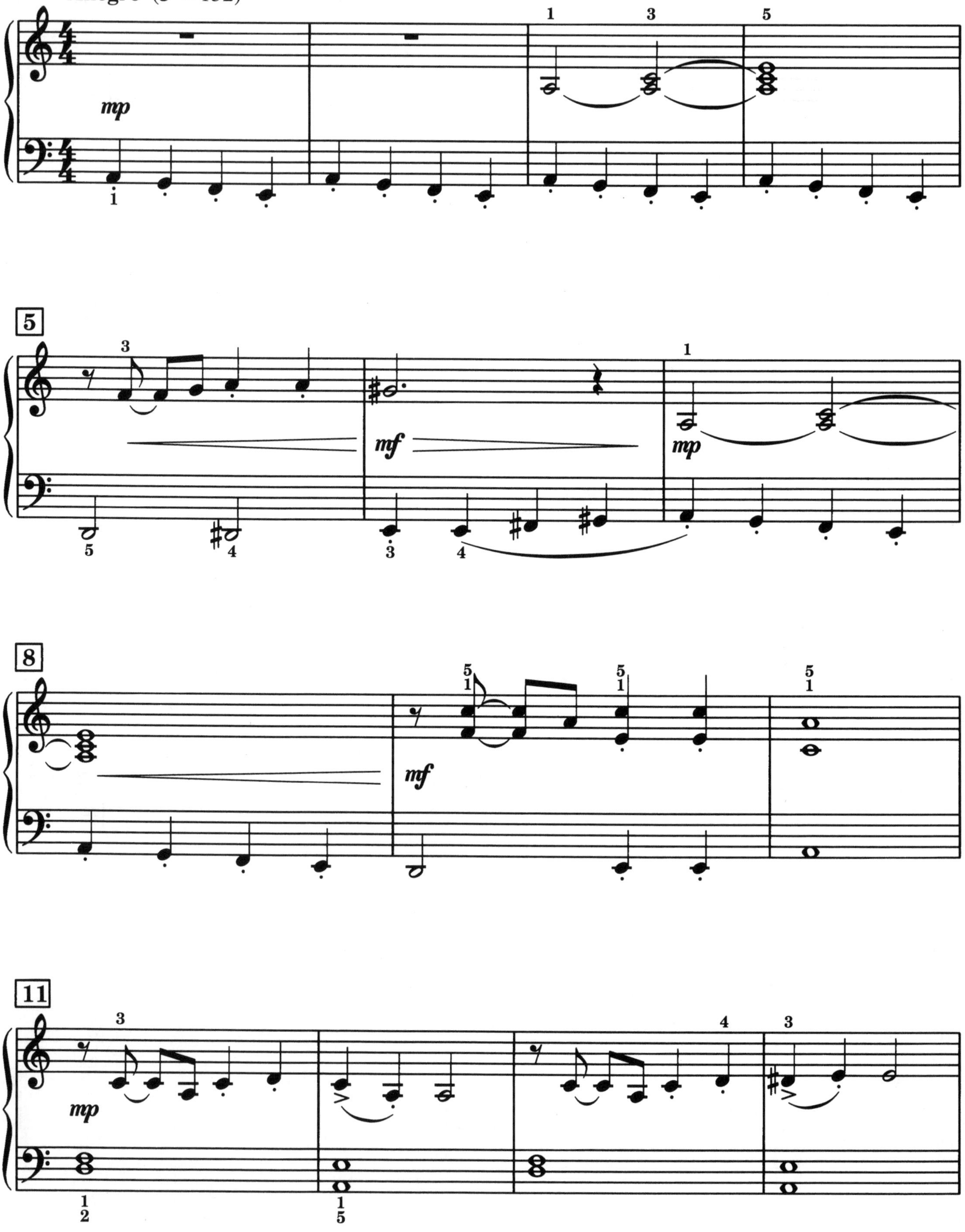

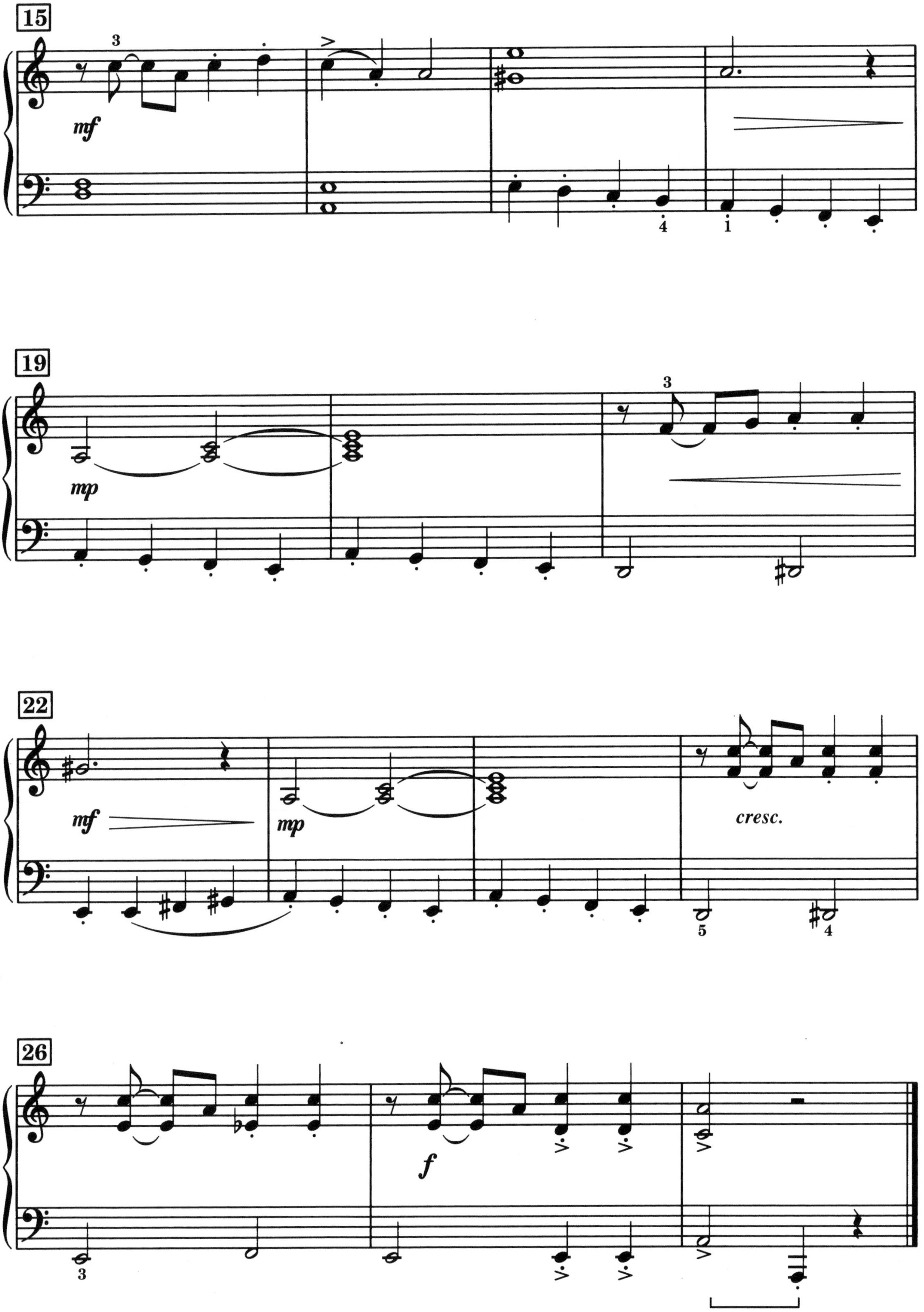
15
mf
19
mp
22
mf
mp
cresc.
26
f

Downright Happy Rag

Bright and bouncy (Play ♫ evenly)

Martha Mier

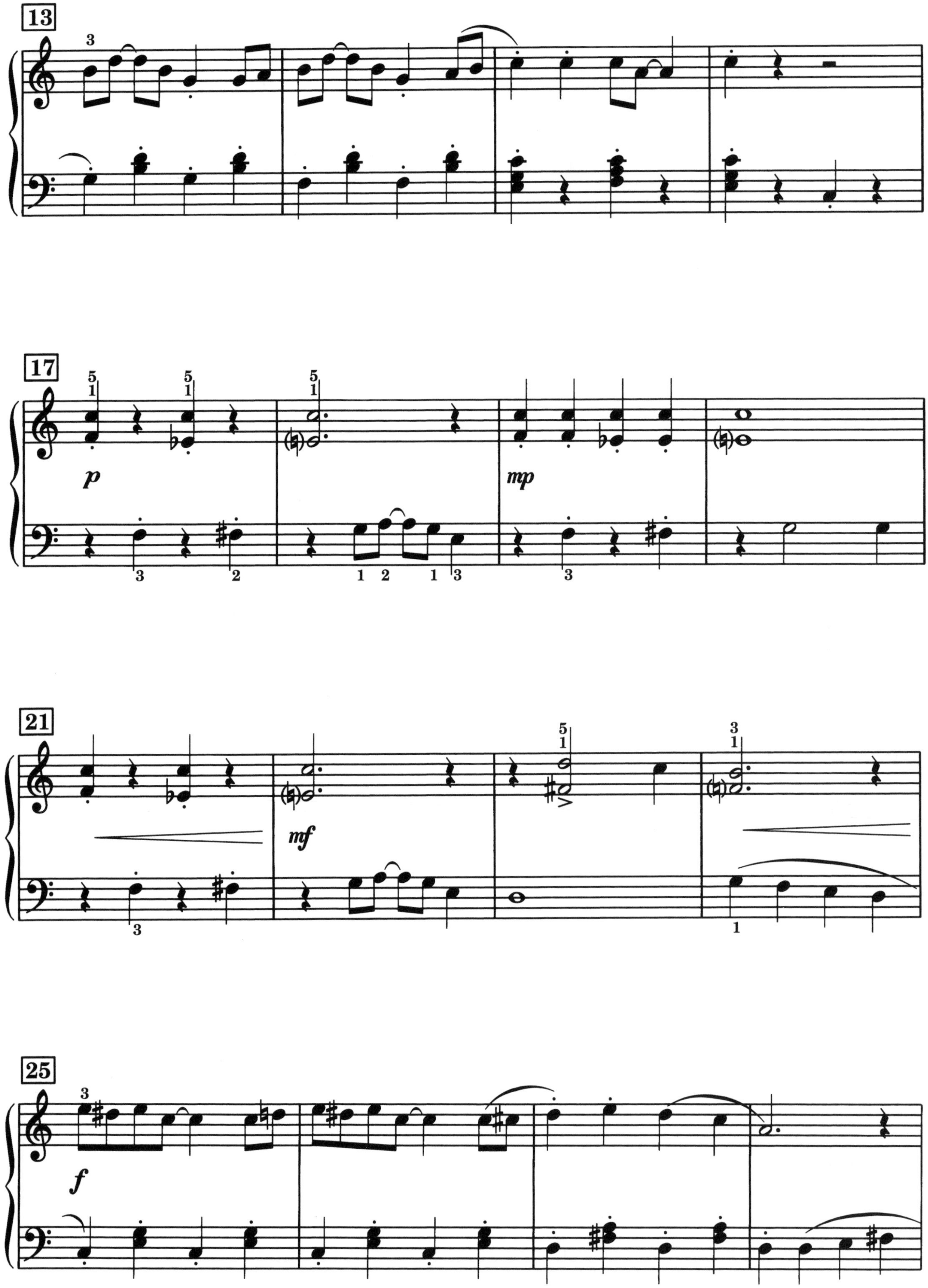
13
17
p
mp
21
mf
25
f

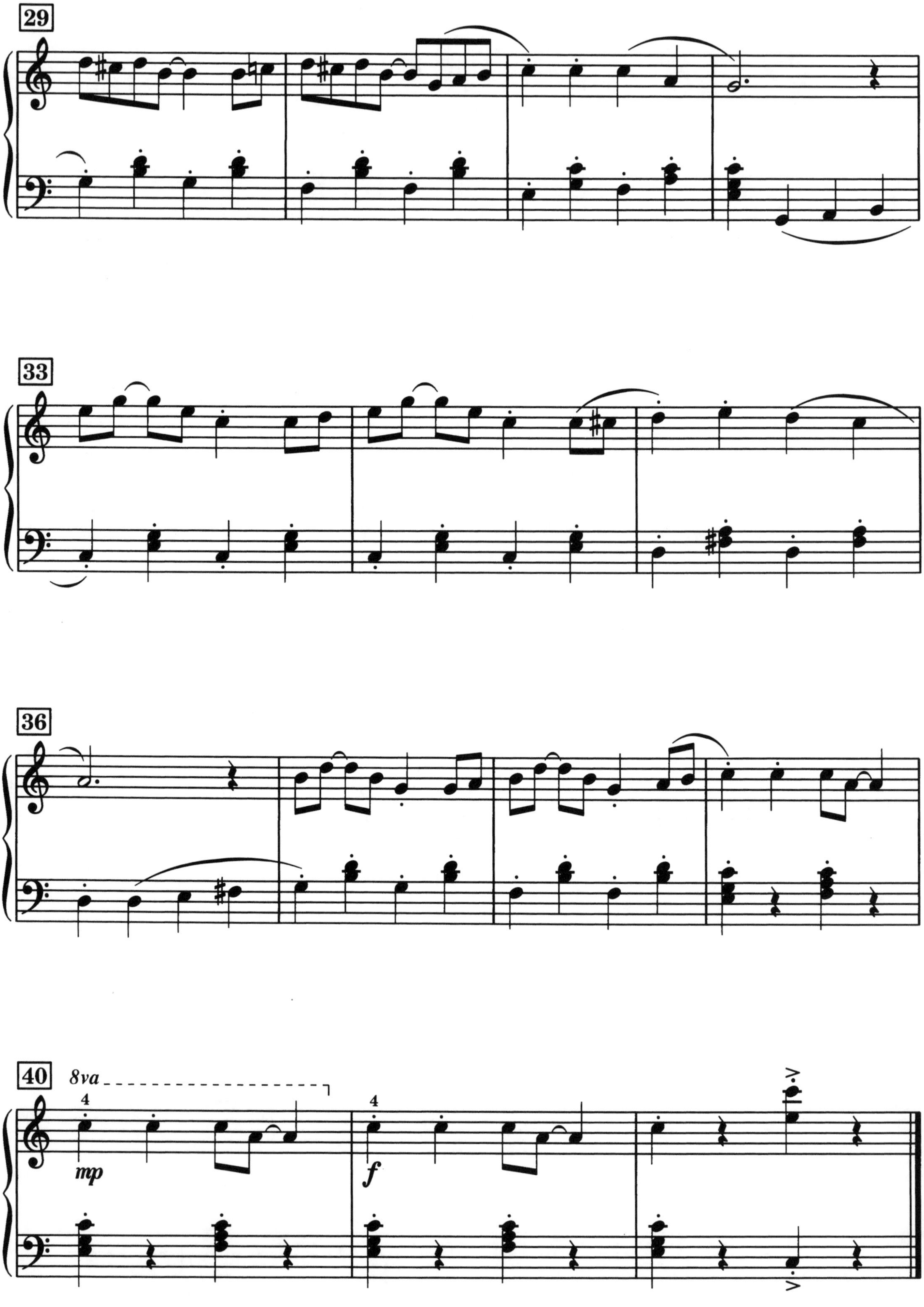
29
33
36
40
8va
4
mp
4
f

A Neat Beat

Martha Mier

Precisely, with a driving beat (♩ = 144)

13
f
17
mp
21
mf
mp
25
cresc.
mf
8va

29
mp
cresc.
32
mf
35
f
38
3
ff
2

Alfred

Martha Mier's Jazz, Rags & Blues Series

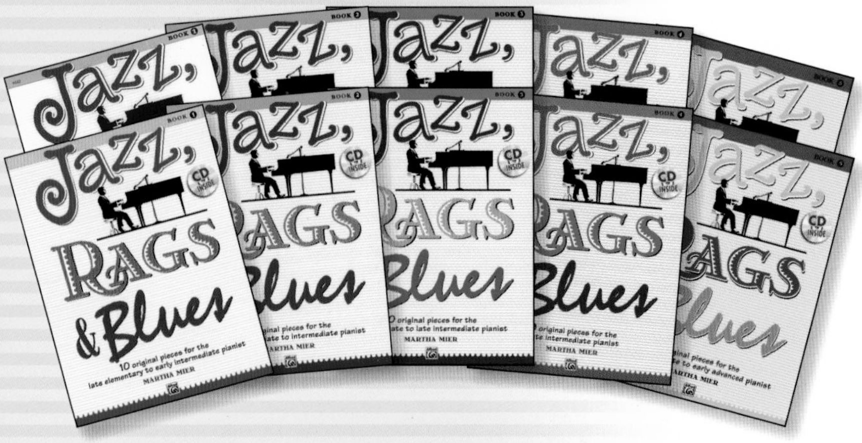

Jazz, Rags & Blues

	Book Alone	Book & CD
Book 1: Late Elementary/Early Intermediate	**6642**	**36721**
Book 2: Early Intermediate/Intermediate	**6643**	**36724**
Book 3: Intermediate/Late Intermediate	**16871**	**36727**
Book 4: Late Intermediate	**18770**	**36730**
Book 5: Late Intermediate/Early Advanced	**32715**	**36733**

CD for Books 1-3 *(rec. Kim O'Reilly)* **18115**

Also available for purchase at alfred.com/downloads

General MIDI

Visit alfred.com/downloads *to purchase MIDI files for books 1-4*

Jazz, Rags & Blues for Two

Book 1: Early Intermediate	**21386**
Book 2: Intermediate	**21387**
Book 3: Intermediate/Late Intermediate	**22454**
Book 4: Late Intermediate/Early Advanced	**22455**
Book 5: Early Advanced	**38829**

Christmas Jazz, Rags & Blues

Book 1: Late Elementary/Early Intermediate	**24435**
Book 2: Intermediate	**22419**
Book 3: Intermediate/Late Intermediate	**26139**
Book 4: Late Intermediate	**26140**
Book 5: Late Intermediate/Early Advanced	**36343**

Classical Jazz, Rags & Blues

Book 1: Early Intermediate	**28987**
Book 2: Intermediate	**28988**
Book 3: Intermediate/Late Intermediate	**31860**
Book 4: Late Intermediate	**31861**
Book 5: Late Intermediate/Early Advanced	**39316**

6642 Book US $7.99

0 38081 02048 8

Alfred

alfred.com

ISBN-10: 0-7390-0963-X
ISBN-13: 978-0-7390-0963-

9 780739 009635 507